T0332138

The

e**X**treme

Middle

Party

The
eXtreme
Middle
Party

Passionately Pragmatic Solutions For:
Health Care, Taxes, Electoral Reform
and more of America's Problems

M. Scott Flood

THE EXTREME MIDDLE PARTY
PASSIONATELY PRAGMATIC SOLUTIONS TO: HEALTH CARE, TAXES, ELECTORAL REFORM AND MORE OF AMERICA'S PROBLEMS

iUniverse books may be ordered through booksellers or by contacting:

iUniverse
1663 Liberty Drive
Bloomington, IN 47403
www.iuniverse.com
844-349-9409

ISBN: 978-1-6632-0806-4 (sc)
ISBN: 978-1-6632-0805-7 (e)

Library of Congress Control Number: 2020916348

Print information available on the last page.

iUniverse rev. date: 09/18/2020

Income inequality has never been greater than it is today in 2020. Ultimately this system is destabilizing for any nation. When 1% have almost everything, 10% live acceptably, and everyone else is struggling or in outright poverty, it is inevitable that society will eventually crumble. The US is getting dangerously close to this level of inequality. And there is a reason most of the money has funneled upward to the very few. The 10 new kitchens parable explains how it happens and how to maintain a vital middle class in a nation.

Ten New Kitchens

〜〜〜〜〜〜〜〜〜〜〜〜〜〜〜〜〜〜〜〜〜〜〜〜〜〜〜〜〜〜〜〜

A Parable

Two brothers, Ronald and Dwight, both very successful businessmen, lived in adjacent nations. Each earned around five million dollars a year, which was 100 times the average salary of $50,000. Ronald lived in Richland, a place where wealth was worshiped and prosperity was supposed to trickle down to the middle class, so taxes on the rich were very low. One year Ronald made an "extra" million dollars. He already easily lived on the first five million, so he decided to spend the bonus million on a fabulous new kitchen. He paid a French chef to consult on the design, he bought specialized German appliances and Japanese cabinetry, he imported the finest marble from Italy and hired a few local workers to do the installation.

Dwight lived over in Fairview. He also made an extra million dollars that year, but people thought differently where he lived. Fairview's folks felt that anyone could live comfortably on 100 times the average salary, so for anything extra after $5 million, the tax rate went to 90%. Dwight knew he would end up paying most of his extra million to the government, so instead he called in his ten best employees and gave each of them a $100,000 bonus that year. Dwight knew he wouldn't have to pay taxes on money he reinvested in his company or gave to his workers. His ten employees would still pay taxes, but at a very low rate, and they could keep almost all of it. What did those ten employees do with the money? Each spent the windfall remodeling their kitchens. They hired local contractors who went to local merchants and purchased the materials needed. They hired ten crews who worked on twelve different projects, employing dozens of people in completing TEN kitchens, not one.

Where do you want to live? Richland or Fairview? Richland is the U.S. today, **Fairview is when the U.S. was great, after WWII, until the disastrous "trickle down" economic theory took hold.**

The take-away from
the Parable

Whenever tax rates are low for the wealthy, money will naturally funnel upward to the few who have the power and the control and the ability to accumulate more and more. From the Roman emperors to the Russian czars to the Chinese dynasties, income inequality always leads to revolutionary movements and eventually the downfall of a nation. Our country is headed down this path today. People seem to think that there's nothing that can be done, but that's untrue. We can return the US to its glory years by returning to the tax system that we had after World War II, when the US middle class was the strongest in the history of the world. Instead of all the money concentrated in a few hands it will be spread to many people, because it will make sense for wealthy business leaders to reinvest profits by rewarding their employees. Instead of money sitting idly in wealthy people's bank accounts or in stock markets, it will be put back into the real economy because middle class people will have it and then spend it.

In our parable, Dwight shared his wealth with his employees not because he's a nice guy, he did it because of the tax system. And the benefits spread far and wide: building 10 new kitchens creates many more good jobs than building one new kitchen. Each project employs many people locally and supports multiple small & medium sized businesses. Each of Dwight's employees buys more at local stores, each kitchen contracting team uses goods and services from the local economy, and all this happens 10 times instead of once. This simple parable applies to all parts of the economy. The middle class is disappearing because our current tax system makes it easy for rich people to hoard their wealth and make their piles bigger and bigger while everyone else gets less and less. We need to return to a much fairer system before it's too late.

And remember, there is a difference between tax policy and tax collected. Today's tax policy with all of its deductions allows the super-rich to keep most of their money. But in Fairview Dwight also didn't pay many taxes. Instead of giving money to the government in the form of taxes, he gave it to his employees in the form of wages. The government still doesn't get the 90%, but the middle class grows strong and as their income increases, so do tax revenues, even at a lower rate.

The XMP proposal for taxes is outlined in chapter 2, if nothing else please take time to read that chapter and then contact your legislators and ask them what they think of the 10 new kitchens tax proposal.

Foreword

As this platform is going to press the United States is in the grips of a worldwide pandemic that has exposed the grievous failings of our government. Our healthcare system doesn't exist. Or at best it can be considered a sick care system. As European nations see their numbers decline our incidence of infection is skyrocketing. Why? Our government is in complete chaos. If our government had a plan in place and good relationships with all other nations, we would have seen this coming and avoided the disaster that ensued. If the XMP system of taxation and healthcare were in effect we would have a robust economy and a healthcare system that could deal with what should have been a manageable situation.

Contents

〜〜〜〜〜〜〜〜〜〜〜〜〜〜〜〜〜〜〜〜〜〜〜〜〜〜〜〜〜〜〜

An extreme overhaul that simplifies tax policy and reduces taxes on the majority
of Americans, while returning rates for the ultra-wealthy to 1950s levels.

Create a three-tier healthcare system that is pragmatic. Provide bare-bones basic
"Medicare for all;" the middle class can purchase additional coverage; and the
wealthy can do whatever they wish. Healthcare also includes death with dignity;
when someone wants to die, let them pass as they wish, with dignity.

End all government payments to the poor and to corporations. If someone is
hungry, give them food not money; if a business can't compete, let it fail. Social
engineering from the left and the right ends.

Re-establishment of the electoral college as a real group that actually meets,
debates and selects the President. Paper ballots for all elections. Re-counts for
all elections, even "landslides." Open primaries.

Enforcement of the 2nd Amendment. Require all states to form well-regulated
militias. Gun owners must be a part of these militias.

Legalize all drugs. Most problems of immigration and crime will disappear.
Reassign money and personnel to fighting other crimes.

For 160 years police around the country have treated black people worse than
white people. Everyone knows this, but nothing ever changes. Institute major
changes forcibly from the outside, via new local, state, and federal rules, so that
cops are finally held accountable like everyone else.

Chapter 1

~~~~~~

Introduction
The eXtreme Middle Party

The founders of this nation were well aware of human nature, which has not changed since then.

Their outline for a nation was radical for the time. We need to rekindle that spirit with passionately pragmatic ideas.

The XMP believes that solutions to America's biggest problems already exist, and that these solutions could be implemented if only we as a society could escape the "Either/Or" dynamic that exists between "liberals" and "conservatives", or between "Democrats" and "Republicans". The XMP also believes that the failure of so-called "moderates" and the so-called "middle" is that these groups lack the courage to support genuinely bold and radical solutions, no matter how obviously practical those solutions are. The XMP supports pragmatic, and yet *radical*, ideas that would clearly benefit the vast majority of Americans, but never seem to gain serious traction.

Most of the XMP's ideas are unlikely to be implemented by politicians who follow the rigid ideologies of the existing party system. Some ideas the XMP supports are popular among the far right, but reviled by the far left. On the other hand, some ideas the XMP supports are popular among the far left, but reviled by the far right. Some ideas are even supported by both extremes but not by the so-called "moderates". The majority of the XMP's platform exists in vast middle space where pragmatic solutions exist, but are rejected because they are too daring and because they don't align with existing political orthodoxy on either side. This is the space the XMP seeks to fill, and XMP will support any candidate of any political affiliation who endorses our policy ideas.

The following program outlines the XMP's core priorities across many policy categories, including Taxes, Health Care, Education, Illegal Drugs, Guns, the Justice System, Welfare, Election Laws, and many more.

Chapter 2

~~~~~~

Taxes

TAX POLICY IS A FUNDAMENTAL
FORCE IN SHAPING SOCIETY

The XMP supports a radical restructuring of income tax policies in line with the lessons of the 10 New Kitchens parable. This reform, however, is not merely about returning income tax rates on the ultra-wealthy to the levels last seen during America's golden era, and thus stimulating mass-reinvestment and wage increases. It is also about a reduction in taxes on everyone else and a massive simplification of the tax code for all individuals and businesses. (See appendix)

The core principles of the XMP personal income tax plan are the following:

1. *Starting at twice the current poverty level, all individual income for the non-ultra wealthy will be taxed at a 10 percent flat rate, period.* This will be a substantial reduction in the tax rate most Americans pay, but ultimately will increase the total

tax collected as wages will rise dramatically and more people will be employed.

2. ***This 10 percent flat rate will hold true across all spectrums of American life, as the XMP also* insists *on the complete elimination of all deductions*.** There will be no deductions for having children, no deductions for charitable contributions to churches and non-profits, no deductions for interest payments, no special interest carve outs of any variety for any reason. The term "tax deductible" will disappear. Our country will be able to afford a 10 percent flat tax thanks to the elimination of this kind of social engineering, and people will go back to making decisions for better reasons than taxation outcomes.

3. ***The 10 percent flat rate applies to ALL INCOME.*** Wages, capital gains, family estates/inheritance, real estate transactions, interest, rental income, etc. 10 percent, no more no less. Any current tax rates on any of these incomes that exceed 10 percent will be eliminated.

4. ***Any income that surpasses 100-times the current average American household income will be taxed at a 90 percent marginal rate.*** The XMP believes that anyone making 100-times the national average is well-off enough. The 90 percent rate also applies to ALL INCOME. Wages, capital gains, family estates/inheritance, real estate transactions, interest, rental income, etc. Any combination therein will be taxed at 90 percent, no more no less, once personal income of any combined variety passes the 100x threshold.

5. ***Calculations on income and tax obligations will be spread out over a 10-year average.*** This will provide some relief for those households not generally over the threshold that come into moderate windfalls, such as from estate inheritances.

6. ***This is not a wealth tax, it is only an income tax.*** Portfolio, real estate, and business valuation increases will not be taxed until assets are liquidated into genuine income.

7. ***The precise official value of what is 100-times the income of the average American household will be reassessed every***

year, and hence the line for the 90 percent marginal tax rate will vary as inflation and economic growth shift the figures.

BUSINESS TAXES

The XMP's perspective on business taxes follow the same principles as the 10 New Kitchens parable, but manifest differently because businesses are naturally in a position to reinvest income into America's economy, and thus should be encouraged to maximize profits. Therefore, corporate income tax will be set at a very low level, to encourage investment and job creation.

The core principles of the XMP corporate tax plan are the following:

8. *Corporate taxes will be set at a 10 percent flat rate*, in line with the national income tax flat rate. This rate applies to all profit-making institutions, be they corporations, LLCs, partnerships, etc.

9. *Only when corporate income is transferred to individuals and becomes personal wealth, and only when the value of those transfers exceeds 100x the national income average, will the 90 percent tax rate listed above come into play.* This applies across all the myriad ways that corporate profits become personal wealth: dividend distributions, executive bonuses, in-kind services, and of course salaries and wages. Other forms of wealth transfers, such as stock options, equity, etc., will only be taxed upon liquidation, as per the personal income tax rules explained above.

10. *Businesses, like individuals, will be granted absolutely no tax deductions whatsoever.* Our country will be able to afford the deeply reduced and simplified 10 percent flat tax rate on our corporations because finally they will all be required to pay taxes.

11. *Genuine non-profit organizations, including religious institutions, will continue to pay no income taxes*, assuming they comply with existing regulations and reinvest all income into their operations and charities. Employees of non-profits will be treated the same as everyone else, taxed at the 10 percent flat rate, and 90 percent for any income that an executive happens to make that exceeds the 100x threshold.

12. *Tax-dodging phony LLCs and individual business licenses used to conceal personal income as business income, and personal spending as business spending, will be banned.* So-called family businesses, limited partnerships, and individuals who declare themselves a business unto themselves, all for the purposes of exceeding 100x income (by hiding that income as "business income") will be subject to severe legal repercussions.

Chapter 3

~~~~~~

Health Care

HEALTH CARE

The XMP takes a pragmatic approach to health care policy, and accepts that the realities of health care costs in the 21st century preclude a perfect solution for everyone. Similarly, although the XMP supports a route to ensuring health care coverage for all Americans, regardless of how poor or rich they are, it is neither realistic, nor feasible, nor even fair to require that all Americans have the same health insurance coverage. The rich are rich, and they will always be rich, and if the rich want to pay for superior health care than everyone else, that is their right. In the meantime, however, some degree of guaranteed universal health insurance should be in place for anyone who wants to access it.

The difference between the XMP's approach to universal health care and the boilerplate approach is that the XMP understands that the United States simply cannot afford to provide truly high quality, entirely universal, fully equal health care to everyone. Medicare-for-all can be a reality, but only if costs stay low. And costs can only stay low if the coverage that Medicare-for-all provides remains within reason.

Therefore, the pillars of the XMP's health insurance policies are the following:

1. *The United States cannot afford to keep everyone alive until they are 100 years old.* This is simply fiscal reality, and health care policy needs to reflect that reality. The ramifications of this reality may prove to be painful at times for some individuals and families, but if America accepts this reality then a baseline of universal socialized health care is possible.

2. *The XMP proposes a three-tiered system of health insurance options:*

    A. **A tax-payer funded, zero-fee Medicare-for-all option for all who want it, which comes with many limitations on coverage and costs.** This free and universally available option will not cover health care services above a certain price range, which will result in unfortunate but necessary tradeoffs and decisions for those who choose to partake. No elective procedures will be covered, no fertility treatments will be covered, no organ transplants will be covered after a certain age, no designer drugs will be provided, generic drugs will be mandated in most circumstances, and very limited elder-care and/or life-extending procedures will be covered after the age of 80. This Medicare-for-all will be affordable for the US and allow its poorest and most vulnerable to always have coverage, and for the young and middle aged, it will cover most health care needs for most people. Many middle class healthy people will opt for this coverage as well, as it will involve zero costs besides the taxes that everyone pays. The coverage would likely include baseline services like health check-ups and follow-ups, common drugs, standard treatment for diseases, pre-natal care, first trimester abortions, prosthetics, orthotics, emergency treatment for accident trauma, and mental health treatment.

B. **Private supplemental insurance for specific scenarios, primarily designed with middle- and upper-middle class consumers in mind.** The private sector will have every opportunity to step in and offer additional coverage for specific gaps in the Medicare-for-all program listed above. Americans of some moderate means will be able to access and leverage these targeted insurance programs to ease their concerns over 'worst-case-scenario' needs (organ transplants, long-term disability, access to non-generic drugs, etc.). Consumers will pay out of pocket for these, or access them via workplace benefits packages. Elder-care insurance options will also likely be a popular choice, although these will likely be very expensive.

C. **Designer, luxury-style private insurance options for the wealthy and ultra wealthy.** As mentioned above, the rich will always be rich and they will always be here, and if they choose to opt out of the above packages in order to ensure world-class care for every conceivable contingency, they may do so. These private policies will likely be outrageously expensive and will probably even involve entirely new private institutions serving only the ultra-wealthy. So be it. But the wealthy will still need to pay Medicare taxes like everyone else.

3. *In some cases, the rich will live and the poor will die.* This is the unfortunate reality of our world, and it is not up to the government to step in and somehow overcome this fundamental unfairness. The costs of doing so would simply be too high, and

would cripple the rest of the economy. The rich have always lived longer than the poor, and they will continue to do so. But the XMP's universal Medicare-for-all baseline option should still improve the quality of life and the financial health of many struggling American families.

4. ***Finally, all Americans will be granted the right to die with dignity.*** Assisted suicide will be legalized on Federal, State, and Local levels, and a series of procedures will be implemented to lower the hurdles and ease the burdens necessary for individuals and families to make this difficult decision. For instance: before the age of 50, a terminally-ill and/or mentally deteriorating and/or overwhelmingly-in-pain patient seeking "death with dignity" via assisted suicide will need authorization from at least two doctors and one psychiatrist; from the ages of 50-70 a patient will only need authorization from one doctor and one psychiatrist; from 70-80 a patient will only need authorization from a psychiatrist; and after age 80 no medical authorization whatsoever will be necessary. This may seem extreme, but the XMP represents the Extreme Middle.

Chapter 4

Welfare

THE WELFARE STATE - SOCIAL AND CORPORATE

The XMP supports a dramatic reduction in public giveaways, to both individuals and corporations. If a person or a business needs public assistance in order to survive, then they haven't figured out how to live and thrive in our system. The government should not be sending free money to either.

For individuals, giving cash, food stamps, vouchers, or other benefits rarely if ever helps improve the lives of the recipients over the long term. *The XMP supports the establishment of an entirely new system for rehabbing, re-educating, re-training — and in the meantime feeding and housing — individuals and families that for whatever reason are not able to survive in our society as it is constituted.* Without regard for how or why a family or individual was unable to make ends meet, those in need should have access to government-sponsored semi-mandatory boarding houses, which double as college campuses and training centers. These boarding houses will be free, will involve intensive training and educational opportunities, will provide childcare and meals, will supply health care (and emphasize mental health treatment), and will entail very strict rules about drug use, alcohol, and general behavior. Life will be highly regimented, and for some it will be partially akin to a prison, but it will be free until families or individuals are able to "graduate" into society via a safe plan for independent living above the poverty line. If the system does not prove able to graduate its clients back into society, the program will be changed again and again until it begins to succeed.

In the corporate world, the government needs to stop picking favorites, and stop bailing out favored corporate constituencies when certain industries or sectors get into trouble. This aid-freeze applies to all federal welfare that flows to agriculture & farmers, manufacturers, financial firms and Wall Street interests. When a company gets into trouble and can't pay for itself anymore, it should face the same fate as any other failure: it must reduce its assets and restructure, or its owners and stakeholders must dissolve and go their separate ways. Similarly, incentive-laden tax breaks for favored corporate investors should be eliminated. This includes banning special deals to provide low-tax or tax-free opportunities to woo companies to move to certain locales, and also banning sweetheart deals for White Elephant projects like sports stadiums and other for-profit social and/or entertainment venues. These issues are admittedly local and not federal, but the XMP will support local and state leaders that align with these positions.

Chapter 5

Electoral Reform

ELECTION LAWS

When the United States was founded, one of the core compromises that allowed the States to Unite was the invention of the Electoral College. The Electoral College was brought into being in order to balance the power among the states when choosing federal leaders. Meanwhile, the Federal Government was designed to oversee the various States, rather than oversee the people. Therefore, at the federal level our system is designed to debate on and balance between the interests of the States, rather than the interests of the people.

Today America continues to grapple with the realities and constraints of this design, which has led to a predictable democratic imbalance wherein low-population States (and their voters) have much more power than high-population States (and their voters). Given that this system is how the Founders intended it, and that it is locked into the Constitution, this imbalance is and will remain a long-term reality. Rather than fighting and resisting the Electoral College, or seeking its elimination, the XMP recommends a rededication to the principles on which it was founded.

The XMP's position on electoral reform is the following:

1. *The Electoral College's stature should be enhanced, and its position and function should return to its original intent*. The Electoral College should once again, quite literally, choose the president. If the Electoral College was doing its job as intended by the Founders, then neither Donald Trump *nor* Hillary Clinton would have ended up as president. Responsible Republican electors would've used their powers the way that Thomas Jefferson had in mind, and blocked the un-qualified populist demagogue. Instead, a qualified, reliable member of the GOP would've gotten the nod.

2. *Similarly, the XMP would like to see the 17ᵗʰ Amendment repealed, and the election of Senators returned to the hands of State Legislatures*. The Founders knew what they were doing when they delegated this power to State government rather than the whims of the people. As with nearly all of the Founders' decisions, these systems were designed to limit the influence of demagogues and extremists, and to make it harder for unqualified and unvetted politicians to rise to positions of power. Returning Senatorial appointments to state governments would also dramatically enhance the importance of state and local elections, driving political awareness back to the level where it most needs to be refocused.

3. *All elections at the county level and above — other than the presidency — must have open primaries*. This process might result in two republicans or two democrats running against each other in the general election, which allows for people from all walks of life and all political ideologies to have a chance at serving in office, rather than only those that serve one or

the other's "base". In the future, open primaries for the White House may also be considered.

4. ***All elections at the county level and above must have paper ballots***. Every election, even a "landslide," will have a paper ballot count which can be crosschecked to prove the result is legitimate.

5. ***Term limit reform is imperative***. Term limits at the federal level should be implemented so as to optimize the balance between valuable experience and the need for 'new blood." The XMP supports the following range of term limits for various positions (*note that the years are not always divisible by existing term lengths, so as to account for partial-term appointments and replacements):
   - House of Representatives - 20 year limit
   - The Senate - 25 year limit
   - The Supreme Court - 25 year limit
   - The Presidency - 10 year limit (which is the existing limit)

6. ***Finally, campaign donations should only come from individual contributors***. No more corporate donations, no more union donations, no more "PACs", no more dark money from 501(c)(4,5,6) advocacy groups. This reform will be a heavy lift, since the Supreme Court believes that corporations are people, and free speech rules protect dark money from the 501 non-profits as well. It may well require a constitutional amendment, but so be it.

Chapter 6

〜✕〜

Guns

GUN RIGHTS AND GUN CONTROL

The Second Amendment to the United States Constitution is one sentence long, and says precisely, "A well regulated Militia, being necessary to the security of a free State, the right of the people to keep and bear Arms, shall not be infringed."

The XMP does not seek to interfere with or re-interpret the intentions of the Constitution's authors, nor does the XMP support taking guns away from those who own them. ***However, it is clear that***

**the direction of gun ownership in this country did not follow the path
that the Founders intended.**

The XMP believes that the Founders supported the idea of well-regulated militias at the local and state level, and we also believe that their concept that gun ownership would be necessary so as to ensure the existence of these militias also makes sense. These militias, as envisioned, were meant to be the ultimate guarantors of American national security, both at the local and national levels. However, in the 21st century the US has ended up with enormous amounts of private gun ownership with little if any public-service or national commitment associated with this ownership. Citizens were meant to keep and bear arms so as to provide collective security — in an *institutionalized* and *well-regulated* manner — but instead gun ownership has evolved into an entirely private concept with little or no obligation to fellow citizens or society.

Thus, the XMP proposes:

1. **The right to gun ownership shall not be infringed, however anyone wishing to own a gun in the US must also belong to a well-regulated militia.** These militias will, at local levels, enforce their own rules and customs regarding training, licensing, participation, background checks, and civic responsibility but they cannot be just for show. Some degree of service hours per week or per month will be obligatory, some militia members will be full-time, and localities and states will provide payment to militia members for this service. In the event of national war — or in the unlikely event of a foreign invasion — these militias will be called upon and their members will be obligated to answer the call.

2. **As the ranks of local and state militias grow, the size of the United States national military will draw down.** As the Founders intended it, local and state militias will be the final guarantors of Americans' freedom and security, and will make up the backbone of a national military if need be. These militias will be defensive in nature, responsive to threats both within and without, and their existence will lessen the need for such a massive national military industrial complex abroad. The

US armed forces have moved disastrously far away from being defensive in nature (which is what the Founders intended), but these 2nd Amendment militias will naturally only be defensive, as they will not be equipped for wild-eyed invasions of foreign countries nor will they be able to act as international policemen. US national security will increase under this vision, even as national spending on military affairs declines, because the security blanket will broaden even as it comes back to a human-level scale.

3. *Villages, cities, counties, and states will be obligated to form these militias, and will be obligated to fund them.* This will add a substantial new security-related expense to local budgets, but tax dollars previously allocated to the US Army, Navy, Air Force, and Marines will be redirected to these local militias. These militias will be akin to a local version of the Coast Guard and the National Guard, which is what the Founders envisioned when they wrote the 2nd Amendment in the first place.

4. *Gun violence in this country will slowly decline as gun owners are obligated to — and are paid to — shift to a service-oriented, public security-oriented, and professionalized militia-style environment.* Again, no one over the age of 18 will be restricted from gun ownership, because the militia itself will be required to accept all citizens that are willing and able to follow the local rules and customs regarding training, licensing, participation, background checks, and civic responsibility. However, if a citizen refuses to join the local militia, then they will not be allowed to own a gun.

5. *The national military will continue to exist, of course, as will all of its branches, but at a substantially reduced headcount, because many soldiers will serve locally and earn salaries locally.* As the taxpayer costs for soldiers are reallocated to local and state levels, and national security is guaranteed via militias across the nation, the national defense department budget will decline. The temptation for endless and hopeless money-draining blood-soaked foreign adventures will decline commensurately.

Chapter 7

Drugs

DRUG POLICY

The decades-long "War on Drugs" has cost our nation billions of dollars, ruined thousands of lives, decimated families, and led us to amass the largest prison population on the planet — all while accomplishing absolutely nothing to halt the spread of illegal drugs. In fact, the only beneficiaries of the endless war have been the for-profit private prisons, the fat budget lines of the government agencies prosecuting the war, and the drug cartels themselves, whose monopolist positions are forever secure under the current policies.

The XMP opposes the War on Drugs as well as nearly every counterproductive drug policy currently in existence in the US. Instead, *we support a policy of radical legalization of all narcotic substances, both soft and hard.* Not just decriminalization; full legalization. So-called "soft" drugs like marijuana should be treated like alcohol, while harder substances should be regulated more rigorously for safety concerns (quality control) — but all of it should be free to manufacture, distribute, sell, and use. Drug makers and dealers will be registered, regulated, and taxed just like any other business, but they will not be prohibited.

Our southern border is crowded with refugees fleeing the violence caused by drug gangs fighting with each other for control of the trade, and our inner cities are riddled with crimes committed by drug dealers trying to control market-share. What's driving all this? The opportunity for profit. And that opportunity only exists because a demand is not being served. If customers (drug users) were able to get their needs fulfilled legally, there would be no profit motive for gangs and criminals, and the violence would dissipate, both in Mexico and the US.

The death toll in the suburbs and rural areas was fueled by the opioid crisis. People got hooked on legal medications and then they were denied further doses. The solution? Make prescription drugs available at cost for everyone. Drug companies can compete with each other on price and quality, and guaranteed access at the neighborhood drug store will dramatically reduce violence. Accidental deaths will decline thanks to quality control, and crime will decline because users will not have trouble getting their fix.

A profit incentive emerges whenever drug use or access is prohibited, and unregulated commerce inevitably falls into the hands of violent market participants. That gap between supply and demand has to be shut, and full legalization is the only solution.

Once the War on Drugs is ended, the huge amount of savings can be re-directed towards dealing with the problem of addiction and its impact on individuals, families, and society. The XMP advocates for:

1. Ensuring the universal availability of ~~cheap~~ affordable or inexpensive (or free) drug treatments for any user who wants help getting clean.

2. Making mental health services much more widely available for drug users so the underlying causes of drug dependency can be addressed.
3. Developing high-speed detection devices for industrial or transit facilities so people who are on drugs can be cited for operating machinery.
4. Establishing living facilities for those who are hopelessly drug dependent, including free counseling and mandatory work requirements. (See chapter on Welfare)
5. Changing our culture so that repeated hard drug use is considered an illness rather than a crime, and is treated as such.

Chapter 8

Racism

RACISM AND POLICE BRUTALITY

The XMP accepts that black people have been at a disadvantage in this country since the beginning, and still are. Slavery is America's original sin, and pervasive racism is its current sin. It is hard, if not impossible, to change people's hearts, but the government can do a better job insuring that formal discrimination (which is already illegal for the most part) is actually punished, and that current laws designed to get the boot off the neck of black and brown folks are actually enforced. Housing and hiring discrimination is already technically illegal in this country, but everyone knows these rules are rarely enforced. Under the XMP, these rules would be intensively enforced, so that everyone has a fair shot.

The XMP does not favor specific rules that provide active favoritism towards any group, race, religion, corporation, etc. Active quota systems, affirmative action, etc., have not been effective and have even engendered greater resentment from America's racists, thus prolonging the era of racial divisions. The XMP does not advocate for more policies along these lines.

That said, there is one area where black people have been overwhelmingly, (and unfairly,) targeted by government persecution for almost all of America's history, and that is the area of policing and law enforcement. Cops in this country have discriminated against black people for so long and so extensively that it has been a subject of comedy routines for literally decades. Black folks suffer from police violence, police brutality and police executions at rates that are so disproportionate to their population that police agencies have to try to hide the data. Fraudulent criminal prosecutions, fake evidence, and false testimony also overwhelmingly target black suspects. Under these circumstances, black people are not truly getting a fair shot in this country. No one should have to live with the kind of fear that this unequal treatment engenders.

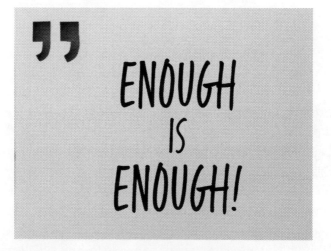

This is an area where government has direct responsibility, and needs to be held accountable, because in this case it is the government that is using its legal authority to facilitate the oppression of one segment of society. **Thus, the XMP favors radical reform within America's police forces.** We do not believe that it is possible for the police to reform themselves from the inside. The police have been beating up black folks for 160 years, in ways that they almost never do, to white folks. For generations police chiefs have been making empty promises to improve, but they never improve. The cops are akin to the Catholic clergy: for thousands of years priests knew that other priests were abusing children, but for thousands of years the "good apples" never exposed the "bad apples", so the "bad apples" never stopped. It is the same with the police: the good guys clearly are unwilling to step up and do what needs to be done. Institutions like the church and the police can't fix themselves, they can only be fixed from the outside.

Thus, the XMP proposes:

1. ***Police officers should no longer have any degree of immunity or special privileges when it comes to accountability for acts of violence.*** Too many states and localities give cops the benefit of the doubt when they assault or kill citizens, even when those citizens are unarmed. Cops should immediately be suspended when they act out violently against unarmed people. If it happens a second time, they should be fired. If they kill someone who was unarmed, they should be arrested immediately. Right now, 99% of cases of police brutality result in no punishment whatsoever, much less jail time. This data point needs to be reversed.

2. ***The records of police officers and police agencies should be public, like they are with every other government agency.*** Too many states and localities allow police to hide the records, backgrounds, and statistics of their officers' behavior, in ways that would never be allowed for teachers or elected officials. Cops are public employees and they should be treated the same as other public employees. So-called "bad apples" can hide behind these secrecy privileges even when they've brutalized dozens of people. All police performance records should be public and transparent.

3. ***The militarization of America's police forces needs to end immediately and be reversed.*** Currently, police forces around the country are loaded up with advanced military weapons, technology, vehicles, etc., which the US Army passes down to them when the army gets new gear. This is why cops can show up looking like Seal Team 6, or like they're in an Avengers movie, when Americans are trying to exercise their constitutional

rights. This relationship between the police and the army needs to end, and the military gear needs to be reclaimed and retired.

4. ***Until America's police are able to purge themselves of the "bad apples" in their ranks, neighborhood policing should be assigned based on race and ethnicity.*** Most police forces don't have enough black and brown officers to ensure that neighborhoods comprising a majority of people of color, are policed by officers of the same race and ethnicity. Therefore, in the near-term, this rule would obligate police agencies to hire a more disproportionate number of minority recruits. The XMP doesn't support affirmative action per se, but this is different. It can't be helped. The cops are too white to keep the peace in a fair and just manner, so the demographics of their ranks need to change.

Chapter 9

Corruption

CORRUPTION

For too long, our public institutions have been abdicating their responsibilities to the nation by selling out their roles to the private sector. This manifests in the form of "privatization" of basic government duties and services, generally under the guise of some ideological notion that the private sector can save the taxpayers money by providing the service in question more cheaply. In reality, this outsourcing is a huge taxpayer-funded giveaway to private corporations, who often have corrupt personal or family connections to the government leaders granting the contracts.

More importantly, this corrupt trend has infiltrated the government's national security, military, and law enforcement responsibilities in ways that transcend mere corruption and cross into the unethical and immoral. *The XMP calls for the immediate end to any private sector government-funded profiteering off of America's foreign wars, and the end to any private-sector security-related presence in war zones.* If any American is going to be armed and authorized to use force in the name of military activities or our national security, that person should be a soldier or an official member of the national security community, and unequivocally be a representative of the United States government. No more private armed security forces abroad, funded by US taxpayers. We have a military for a reason; if dirty work, unpleasant work, or even inefficient work needs to be done in the name of military operations, that is the job of the armed services. If anyone is going to be paid for that work, it should be soldiers and official support staff, not corrupt millionaire defense contractors with zero accountability. These contractors only make money if America remains forever at war. They need to be cut off.

Secondly, just as importantly, *the XMP calls for the end to all privatization of America's prison systems, justice system, and law enforcement.* In a democracy we as citizens grant our government the right to implement law enforcement, judicial systems, and (when necessary) incarceration facilities. These are *not* jobs for the private sector. And it is outrageous that in some cases, particularly with regard to prisons, corrupt millionaire fat-cats are profiteering off our society's addiction to mass incarceration. Private policing is still relatively rare, but given the "privatization" trend overtaking our corrupt politicians, it won't be long before privatizing more cops will be seen as a way to "save money".(.") In reality, any such offloading is an abdication of the government's sacred civil duties and a fat giveaway to favored business leaders — most of whom line the pockets of politicians with campaign finance donations.

When the private sector becomes deeply entwined with military operations, prisons, policing, etc., then their profits rely on

ever-more military operations, ever-more prisons, and ever-more policing. It doesn't take a rocket scientist to understand what policy outcomes these companies will push for in the future.

It is also not true that the private sector can always accomplish policy goals more cheaply than government agencies. Private corporations often come in with promises of much lower rates, but rarely deliver ~~by~~;; the end. Cost overruns and delays result in total billing being the same as it would have been before, except after privatization the regular workers get much less money, and the owners pocket all the extra funding. At least a slow and bloated government project run by the actual government involves good paychecks for middle class employees doing the work. The private companies can offer "cheaper" services because they pay employees so much less; and then they fail to deliver the lower costs and higher quality regardless. But these deals keep happening, because the corruption and ideology is entrenched.

This trend towards private profit off of public resources extends to other topics; such as, the Western part of our nation is opening up public lands for exploitation by billionaires, essentially a totally free giveaway to any corporation with the right corrupt relationships. Meanwhile, low-quality private schools and crappy educational services companies are extracting taxpayer-funded benefits that should be going to actual public schools. Regardless of whether our public schools are doing a good job or not (many, granted, are not), there's no reason to shift our taxpayer money directly into the pockets of private-player scam artists pretending to offer magic education solutions. Yet this is happening on a daily basis, mainly because of corrupt political relationships.

The XMP calls for a vast, sweeping review of all such government outlays related to "privatizing" or "outsourcing" government responsibilities like education, environmental protection, prisons, military operations, and national security. Any such privatization in war zones or in association with active military operations shall be banned outright; any private prisons shall be banned as well; and the other issues shall receive careful scrutiny and taxpayer outlays shall be much reduced.

Chapter 10

〰〰〰〰〰〰〰〰〰〰〰〰〰〰〰〰〰〰〰〰〰〰

Public Service

PUBLIC SERVICE

American society has always been deeply fragmented, but these cracks and divisions are more noticeable than ever now that we are all interconnected online but not interconnected in real life. Most of these divisions are hopelessly entrenched among existing generations, but there is hope for the future if young people are given the opportunity to break the cultural and economic silos of modern life and form bonds with each other across races, ethnicities, religions, etc. This can be accomplished in such a way that not only increases understanding and harmony, but also strengthens the fabric of national identity and American unity.

For several generations young people have gone directly from high school to college or to the work force. For several reasons, this has not proven to be an optimal choice for 18-year-olds. People of that age have had limited life experience, limited exposure to alternative ideas and possibilities, and usually have very little idea of what they want to do with their lives. Not only that, but this transition moment is also the core point at which American lives tend to become permanently disconnected from experiences outside their own funnel.

Given these two realities, **the XMP proposes a new mandatory universal two-year public service program for young people.** This service will involve obligatory cross-cultural, cross-economic, cross-geographic, and cross-ethnic groupings. If the young person wishes, this service can be in the military, which is arguably the only American institution where such cross-connectivity already exists. However, there will be many other options as well, akin to AmeriCorps, or a range of other regional and national volunteer organizations. **The only rule is that the service time cannot be fulfilled in one's home town.** (Note that religiously affiliated programs will not be allowed unless the organizers are rigorously dedicated to ensuring the majority of the young people involved are not from that particular religion, and the organizers strictly ban proselytizing.)

These programs will bring young people into contact with peers who were raised under very different circumstances than their own. Teenagers will learn how to work together, how to follow a program and a system, how to cooperate, how to listen, how to communicate, and how to give of themselves for a bigger cause. After two years, every young person will have met and generated friendships with numerous people of vastly different backgrounds, and they will have made a positive difference for their country. The public service role will not be a paid position, but there will be stipends to offset lost income for those who are poor and otherwise would need to work to help their families. And all costs will be covered by the federal government for all participants during those years (housing, food, travel, etc.).

This service can be delivered in the cities or in the countryside or anywhere in between. Participants will also learn valuable and practical skills like carpentry, agriculture, nursing, counseling, mechanics, waste clean-up, teaching, etc. The list is endless because the need is massive. The young people will benefit, but so will the country.

Chapter 11

~~~~~~

Climate Change

CLIMATE CHANGE

Anyone who isn't completely blinded by ideology can tell that the climate is changing. Every year we set new records for heatwaves, every year rain and weather patterns get more erratic and unfamiliar, every year the agriculture industry suffers in new and confounding ways, and every year new and greater weather-induced natural disasters hit our country.

It may already be too late to do anything about climate change, but at the very least *the XMP demands that the US government officially declare that climate change is real, climate change is an emergency, and climate change requires immediate action*. Climate change deniers have no place in the XMP or the US government.

The XMP also advocates for less arguing about who or what caused (and is causing) climate change, and more attention for how to mitigate its consequences. It has become clear that human beings around the world are not going to change their behavior in sufficient numbers to ward off the worst of climate change. Even in countries where everyone accepts the truth of climate change, emissions reductions have been paltry. In developing countries, the situation is even worse. Billions of people in India and China have not yet reached the level of economic development of Americans, and they are not going accept rules that say they cannot use fossil fuels the way that Americans always have.

Therefore, the US needs to spend its time and effort preparing for how climate change will create a more dangerous and difficult world for all of us, and less time trying to convince people not to drive cars or eat meat.

Thus, the XMP endorses the following priorities:

1. *Accept the inevitability of rising sea levels, and implement new policies to this affect.* Ban new developments on low-laying shore lines. Cease rebuilding beaches when they are wiped out by weather events. Eliminate federal flood insurance for anything in climate change danger zones. Consult with Dutch engineers on best practices for city-wide sea walls, and begin construction immediately around America's cities that lie too low near ocean fronts.

2. *Ensure the military is planning for downside climate change contingencies.* The US military needs to relocate all bases that are too close to sea level, and reengineer all naval bases and facilities to ensure they can continue to operate even with much higher sea levels. Airports (both civilian and military) are frequently right on shorelines, and these need to be moved. Road and rail infrastructure that is vital for both national security and economic security needs to be moved away from these flood zones as well. All of this will need to be done eventually; it will be cheaper to do it now, in advance.

3. *Tax carbon, because maybe we can slow down the onset of the worst scenarios.* A tax on carbon (and methane) producing

activities won't solve the problem, but it could incrementally improve the situation by staving off near-term worst-case scenarios. If there's a price associated with this kind of business, and even some of corporate America moves away from emissions-heavy industries, then we might slow the melting and buy ourselves some more time for mitigation activities. The tax will also help fund the necessary infrastructure changes.

Chapter 12

~~~~~~

The List Goes On

The preceding pages have outlined the XMP's baseline position on its initial set of priorities, but there are many more vital issues confronting our nation. The list is nearly endless, and some of the problems are of equal importance to those that we have already addressed. Our intention is to make this first book readable, and not overwhelm anyone with too much information or too many ideas.

We also are very eager to hear from our readers and potential supporters about additional ideas, both on the topics we have covered and on new ones.

As time goes on, we will develop more policy positions on topics related to:

- *Abortion rights.* What is the right balance between a women's constitutional right to an abortion and to control her own body, vs. the painful reality of late-stage pregnancies and viable fetuses?
- *Education.* How can we get our middle and high schools to perform up to the level of our relatively strong elementary schools and our world-leading colleges and universities? Is it time to rethink classroom learning entirely and move towards technology-enabled individual teaching? It's definitely time to deemphasize "college-for-all" and reemphasize technical apprenticeships, trade schools, and two-year programs.
- *Sex, gender, and sexual orientation.* How do we ensure that people of all sexual identities get just as much of a fair shot as anyone else, and don't have to walk through life in constant fear for their personal safety, or of losing their job or their home?

The XMP doesn't want anyone to get special treatment, but discrimination is not acceptable no matter what, and a lot of LGBTQ folks face constant discrimination.

- *Social media and fake news.* You can't yell "FIRE!" in a crowded theater, despite the First Amendment, because it is dangerous and causes chaos. At what point does freedom of speech take a backseat to the need to keep our country from falling apart? When does lying online cross a red line and become so dangerous that society can't tolerate it anymore? How do we regulate the private internet companies that facilitate all this and allow it to be anonymous?

- *The gig economy and the new age of work.* How do we embrace the new reality of workforces and job opportunities while still ensuring people are treated fairly?

- *Declarations of war.* The War Powers Act must be repealed. No American soldiers should be sent anywhere in the world without prior approval from Congress. Congress has abdicated its solemn duty, and this duty must be reclaimed, or we will always be in endless forever-wars costing us trillions and accomplishing nothing.

And more and more…

Foreign affairs: counterterrorism, endless wars in the Middle East, our relationship with China, how to deal with dictatorships, how to deal with friends, how much to care about human rights issues abroad, how to create a fair global trading system

Immigration: finding the right balance, fairness at the borders, importing talent vs. preserving jobs for citizens, keeping the best foreign students here (or not), enforcing the rules among employers instead of just workers

Privacy: government collection of personal data (NSA, CIA, FBI, etc.); private companys' collection of personal data (Facebook, Google, Apple, Amazon); what if any is acceptable and how much is too much

Emergency medical preparedness: how to prepare for the next pandemic; how to balance personal liberty vs. the need for public safety during health emergencies; how to ensure the US can manufacture its own supplies of PPE and pharmaceuticals domestically; how to ensure demagogues cannot politicize our scientific and health agencies

Etc., etc., etc. ...

Please send us your solutions to some of the problems above as well as any ideas regarding the topics covered in previous chapters to Info@ ExtremeMiddleParty.com. Also, visit our website ExtremeMiddleParty. com and our page on Facebook.

Appendix

≈≈

These charts show how the highest tax rate has plummeted in parallel with the destruction of the middle class and general decline of our nation. The XMP tax plan would have two rates: 10% and 90% with the 90% rate starting when individual income exceeded 100 times the average income for that year. This figure varies depending on who is included in the "count" but for now, we are using $50,000 which would mean the first 5 million dollars would be taxed at 10% and any earnings above would be taxed at 90%. Remember, NO DEDUCTIONS. Also, no classifications such as head of household, married filing jointly or separately, etc.

Federal – 1957 Single Tax Brackets		Federal - 1984 Single Tax Brackets		Federal - 2019 Single Tax Brackets	
Tax Bracket	Tax Rate	Tax Bracket	Tax Rate	Tax Bracket	Tax Rate
$0.00+	20%	$0.00+	0%	$0.00+	10%
$2,000.00+	22%	$2,300.00+	11%	$9,700+	12%
$4,000.00+	26%	$3,400.00+	12%	$39,475+	22%
$6,000.00+	30%	$4,400.00+	14%	$84,200+	24%
$8,000.00+	34%	$6,500.00+	15%	$160,725+	32%
$10,000.00+	38%	$8,500.00+	16%	$204,100+	35%
$12,000.00+	43%	$10,800.00+	18%	$510,300+	37%
$14,000.00+	47%	$12,900.00+	20%		
$16,000.00+	50%	$15,000.00+	23%		
$18,000.00+	53%	$18,200.00+	26%		
$20,000.00+	56%	$23,500.00+	30%		
$22,000.00+	59%	$28,800.00+	34%		
$26,000.00+	62%	$34,100.00+	38%		
$32,000.00+	65%	$41,500.00+	42%		
$38,000.00+	69%	$55,300.00+	48%		
$44,000.00+	72%	$81,800.00+	50%		
$50,000.00+	75%	$200,000.00+	50%		
$60,000.00+	78%				
$70,000.00+	81%				
$80,000.00+	84%				
$90,000.00+	87%				
$100,000.00+	89%				
$150,000.00+	90%				
$200,000.00+	91%				

Printed in the United States
By Bookmasters